On Jesus' Team
Children's Object Lessons

Wesley T. Runk

C.S.S. Publishing Co., Inc.
Lima, Ohio

ON JESUS' TEAM

6838 / ISBN 0-89536-809-9

PRINTED IN U.S.A.

TABLE OF CONTENTS

Foreword   5

Reward   *Matthew 5:1-12*   7
Solid as a Rock   *Matthew 16:13-19*   9
The Warning Flag   *Matthew 23:34-39*   11
This One's Better   *Mark 1:4-11*   13
Forty Long Days   *Mark 1:12-15*   15
He Knows What He's Talking
    About   *Mark 1:21-28*   17
Traveling Light   *Mark 1:29-39*   19
It's Official   *Mark 1:40-45*   21
God is the Only One   *Mark 2:1-12*   23
Right Way, Wrong Way   *Mark 2:23-28*   25
On Jesus' Team   *Mark 3:20-35*   27
It Just Grows and Grows   *Mark 4:26-34*   29
Sound Asleep   *Mark 4:35-41*   31
Where the Power Is   *Mark 5:21-24a,*   33
                                    35-43
What a Leader   *Mark 6:30-34*   35
Check Inside   *Mark 7:1-8,*   37
                                    14-15, 21-23
You Can't Hold it Back   *Mark 7:31-37*   39
The Most Important Decision   *Mark 8:27-35*   41
Give it Away   *Mark 8:31-38*   43
"Your Attention, Please"   *Mark 9:2-9*   45
"Me First"   *Mark 9:30-37*   47
Room for Difference   *Mark 9:38-50*   49
Keep it Simple   *Mark 10:2-16*   51
Servants are Important   *Mark 10:35-45*   53
No More Begging   *Mark 10:46-52*   55
Roll Out the Red Carpet   *Mark 11:1-10*   57
It's Not Far Away   *Mark 12:28-34*   59
A Great Day   *Mark 16:1-8*   61
Extra Special   *Luke 1:39-45*   63
Making Our Love Increase   *Luke 1:46-55*   65
"I'm Sorry"   *Luke 3:1-6*   67
The Most Important Part   *Luke 3:7-18*   69
He Will Take Care of Us   *Luke 21:10-19*   71
Jesus is Coming   *Luke 21:25-36*   73

A Heap of Blessings	*John 1:1-18*	75
"The Church Store"	*John 2:13-22*	77
Brand New Lives	*John 3:1-17*	79
Darkness and Light	*John 3:14-21*	81
The Very Last Day	*John 6:41-51*	83
Food From Heaven	*John 6:24-35*	85
Living Forever	*John 6:51-58*	87
What Keeps Us Running	*John 6:60-69*	89
God's Good Gift	*John 7:37-39*	91
Jesus Knows	*John 10:11-18*	93
Share It or Lose It	*John 12:20-33*	95
Vines and Branches	*John 15:1-8*	97
Chosen by the Captain	*John 15:9-17*	99
Guarding Us From Evil	*John 17:11b-19*	101
Who's In Charge?	*John 18:33-37*	103
"Prove It"	*John 20:19-31*	105

Foreword

What child doesn't love to hear a story?

These short "parables-from-life" are based on Gospel scripture texts, and are designed to be presented by the pastor or a worship leader, either at the worship service or at Sunday church school, vacation Bible school, or children's worship time. Each makes use of some common, everyday items.

None of the messages are intended to be presented just as they are written. In fact, none of us *talk* the way we *write.* The storyteller will want to read the Scripture text and the story and (if necessary) rehearse it, until it can be presented in a natural story-telling way.

Often tellers of children's messages forget that they are speaking, *not to the adults* who also happen to be present (even though the adults properly are "overhearing" everything), but that, first and primarily, the message is a message *to the children* who are gathered in the chancel, or wherever the story is being told. The story-teller will want to be certain that the youngest child who comes to listen can understand what is being said. If eyes and hands begin to stray, make it simpler still, and, perhaps, be prepared to depart from your "learned script" long enough to regain every youngster's attention.

Now, get ready to invite the youngsters, and to say, "Good morning, boys and girls . . ."

Reward!

Matthew 5:1-12

Rejoice and be glad, for your reward is great in heaven, for so men persecuted the prophets who were before you. (v. 12)

Object: *An ad in the daily newspaper that offers a reward for return of a pet.*

Good morning, boys and girls. How many of you have ever received a reward for doing something? *(Let them answer.)* Was it for something good or was it for doing something bad? *(Let them answer.)* It was for doing something good. That's interesting. When you do something especially good you receive a reward. You don't get a reward for just doing good, but when it is special, you may get a reward.

I have with me this morning a bit of our town's newspaper that talks about a reward for finding a pet. Someone lost their pet and they called the newspaper to have them put this note in that said this, "Reward: Lost dog. German Shepherd, answers to name of Pal, grey and black color. Please call 229-1787."

Someone lost a very nice dog and they want their pet back and are willing to give a reward to anyone who finds him and calls them about the dog. If you found the dog and called them, they would give you a reward. It might be money or something else nice that you would really like. People give rewards for helping them or for doing things that they need to have done. I hope that someone finds Pal and calls them at the number in the paper.

Jesus talked about rewards also. One day he was preaching to a lot of people, and he told them what it was like to be a Christian and follow him. It wasn't easy. As a matter of fact, he warned the people that to follow him would be very difficult, but he said it was worth it. Jesus told them to follow his teachings and the reward would be given to them in heaven. That meant that it had to be good.

The same thing is true for us today. We are also asked to follow Jesus and to do the things that he wants us to do. It may not be easy. It will probably be hard, but it is worth it. Our reward is also in heaven and is part of the promise that Jesus made to us.

I know that Jesus will keep his promise and give us our reward, because he has kept all of his other promises. I believe that someone who lost his dog will give me the reward if I find him. If I believe that people will keep promises and give rewards, then I know that God will do the same and even better.

The next time that you hear about a reward, I want you to think about the time you heard that Jesus also gives rewards; only the reward that we are going to get is a reward when we live in heaven. Amen.

Solid as a Rock

Matthew 16:13-19

You are Peter, a stone, and upon this rock I will build my church, and all the powers of hell shall not prevail against it. (v. 18)

Object: *A stone.*

Good morning, boys and girls. Has anybody ever called you a rock? *(Let them answer.)* Seriously, has anyone ever said to you, "Jim, you are a rock!" or "Mary, you remind me of a rock!" *(Let them answer.)* What does that sound like when someone calls you a rock? Does it sound like they are calling you a bad name, or are they trying to be nice? *(Let them answer.)* Take a look at the rock that I have with me this morning and think about it for a moment. Jesus called Peter, his apostle, a rock. What do you think Jesus meant when he called Peter a rock?

This was a very big moment in Peter's life, and one that he never forgot and neither did any other of the disciples of Jesus. Jesus said, "You are Peter, a stone; and upon this rock I will build my church; and all the powers of hell shall not prevail against it." Does that sound like Jesus was mad at Peter or sad with Peter? I think it sounds like Jesus thought that Peter was strong, and maybe even more. Jesus had asked Peter who he thought he was. Peter replied, "You are the Christ, the Son of the Living God." No one had ever said it that way to Jesus before. Some people had thought about it, and some had wondered about it, but no one ever said that Jesus was something that wonderful. People were afraid to say it. No other man was that great to be called the Son of God. But Peter knew that Jesus was and he said it.

Now Jesus told Peter that it was that kind of faith that was going to build a new church. This church was not going to be like any other church, because it was going to be a church that believed that Jesus was the Christ, the Son of God. Jesus wanted his church to be strong. That is why Jesus said that the church would be built on a rock. Is there anything as solid as a rock? Believing in Jesus and saying so takes great belief and strength. You can build a great house on a rock, It won't cave in, or sink into the ground. A house built on a rock will stand forever as far as the rock on which it is built is concerned.

The next time that you see a rock, you can think about the time that Jesus called Peter a rock and told him that he was going to build his church on a faith like Peter had that day and many days after that day. A rock is the sign of strength. Your faith in Jesus should be as strong as a rock. Then your faith will be like Peter's. Amen.

The Warning Flag

Matthew 23:23-39

Truly, I say to you, all this will come upon this generation. (v. 36)

Object: *A red flag.*

Good morning, boys and girls. I brought with me this morning a flag to share with you. *(Show them the flag.)* How many of you have ever seen a flag like this? *(Let them answer.)* Do you know what country has a flag like this? Is it the American flag? We call the Russians "Reds," so do you think that this may be their flag? *(Let them answer.)* Maybe it isn't the flag of any country. Do you know what else a flag like this could be used for? *(Let them answer.)* I'll tell you what this red flag is used for and I hope you remember it from now on. This is a warning flag. Whenever you see a red flag like this one, it is telling you to beware of danger. Sometimes you will see them on the backs of trucks carrying something too long to fit on the truck. Sometimes you will see a man waving a red flag to tell cars to slow down, because there is something dangerous up ahead. A red flag is a "warning."

In the Bible, Jesus tried to give us some warnings. He did not wave a red flag, but he did tell us that we should know that some people did not love Christians, and that they would cause us great harm. People who live on hate and jealousy try to stop people from being Christians. Jesus knew how men filled with sin would try to stop people from doing good for their neighbors, He knew that they might even kill Christians or try to harm them in some way, if they thought that they could stop people like you and me from following Jesus.

There was a man whom the people of hate did kill, and his name was Stephen. He was one of the early followers of Jesus, and he did many good things for the people of God. He was a great man and he loved people and cared for them every day. Men who hated Jesus and his teachings also hated Stephen, and they finally killed him on the streets in Jerusalem. Jesus told us that things like this would happen, and while he did not wave a red flag to warn us, he still said that we should know that some people would even kill, if they thought it would stop Christianity from growing.

We must still teach about God and Jesus to everyone, but we should not be surprised if some people do not like us and will not follow Christ. There will be some who will laugh and make fun of Jesus, but since we know it, we will not be surprised. When you see a red flag, remember that Jesus warned us, and then be careful but still be loving to everyone as God has taught us. Amen.

This One's Better

Mark 1:4-11

"I baptize you with water, but he will baptize you with God's Holy Spirit!" (v. 8)

Object: *A pen and a pencil.*

Good morning, boys and girls. I brought along with me this morning a couple of items that I am sure you are familiar with and even use a lot. *(Show them the pencil and pen.)* Do you know what these are? That's right. Which one is the pencil and which one is the pen? Very good. You got it right. Now, the next question is, what do we use them for? *(Let them answer.)* That's right, we use them to write with. Both of them write, but one of them, we think, is better than the other. Do you know which one most people think is better than the other one? *(Let them answer.)* That's right, the pen. A pen is more permanent. That means that whatever you write with a pen will last longer than if you write it with a pencil.

John the Baptizer knew that something was different about Jesus from other men. John also knew there was something really different between Jesus and him. Both of them talked about God and preached to the people. Both of them baptized people who had sinned against God. But John said there was a real difference between the baptism that he made, and the one that Jesus made. The baptism by Jesus was better, John said, because when Jesus baptized it was more than just the forgiving of sin. It also meant that you became a part of God's family. His baptism was special; it lasted longer since it was forever.

In other words, when John baptized, it was like writing a note with a pencil. You could read it and know what it meant. But when Jesus baptized, you could not only read it now, but it was like writing with a pen, for it lasts forever.

That is the way John said it. Many people thought that John was like Jesus, but John said that this was not true. John was a special messenger that God sent to introduce Jesus to the world, and tell the world how special Jesus was.

The next time you look at a pencil, or write with one, you can think to yourself that the pencil reminds you of John. He could do a lot of the things that Jesus did, but they were not quite as powerful as the things that Jesus did. When you look at a pen, I hope you will think of Jesus and know that a pen is very special to write with, and will last a long time. When Jesus did something, it lasted forever. Amen.

Forty Long Days

Mark 1:12-15

And he was in the wilderness forty days, tempted by Satan; and he was with the wild beasts; and the angels ministered to him. (v. 13)

Object: *As many small calendars as you can get with the forty days crossed out.*

Good morning, boys and girls. How many of you have a calendar at home? How many of you have a calendar at school? Just about anywhere you go, you can see a calendar hanging or sitting somewhere in the room. I see them in stores and offices and almost everywhere I look. People like to know what day it is, and how many days it will be until they must do something. People keep calendars to remind them of birthdays and other important things that they want to celebrate. What day do you like best that is shown on the calendar? *(Let them answer.)* All of us like certain days and we keep track of them on the calendar.

I brought the calendar with me this morning for another reason. I brought it to show you how long it would take to wait for forty days. Does forty days sound like a long time to you? *(Let them answer.)* How long is forty days? Is it as long as a year? Is it longer than a week? Is it longer than a month? Forty days is a long time. Now, it depends on where you are during those forty days and what you are doing that makes the time go fast or go slow. If you are on vacation and swimming and playing every day, the time goes fast. But if you are doing a hard job or waiting for something important to happen to you, then the days seem to go by very slowly.

The forty days that I am talking about this morning, the ones that I marked on the calendar, are the forty days that Jesus spent in the wilderness. The wilderness is like a desert, and it is a pretty awful place to spend much time. It can be very hot in the daytime and very cold at night. There are no trees, but a lot of rock. There are wild animals that are always looking for something to eat. There is very little growing in the wilderness, and if you did not take a lot of food with you when you went, you would get very hungry.

Jesus lived in the wilderness for forty days and met the Devil every day. The Devil tempted him every day. He tried to get Jesus to do things his way and to be like him. Jesus turned the Devil down every time. It was almost like a war between two people. The Devil tried to make Jesus commit sin and turn against God, but he could not. For forty days, Jesus tested his strength against this evil person and he finally won.

We remember that time by marking our calendars and thanking God for sending us Jesus. With Jesus' help we can defeat the Devil also, but we need Jesus to tell us how and to help us fight against him.

Take your calendars home and mark the days, and see how long Jesus met the Devil every day and how long it took him to win against that evil one. Amen.

He Knows What He's Talking About

Mark 1:21-28

The congregation was surprised at his sermon because he spoke as an authority, and didn't try to prove his points by quoting others — quite unlike what they were used to hearing! (v. 22)

Object: *Ten blue marbles and one green marble.*

Good morning, boys and girls. I have a little experiment to show you this morning that I hope will tell you something about Jesus. This is the experiment. I have eleven marbles and they are all the same in most ways. One of the marbles is the leader of the other ten marbles. I am not going to tell you which one of the marbles is the leader, but I am going to let you pick the leader out. *(Take out the marbles and lay them on the floor, counting them one by one as you show them to the children.)* Now, take a very close look at the marbles and when you think you know which marble I think is the leader, raise your hand. *(Act very surprised when they all raise their hands.)* Which one do you think is the leader? *(Let them answer.)* Why do you think the green marble is the leader? *(Let them answer.)* Because it is the only green marble and all of the rest are blue. There is only one green marble. That's very good, and it is also the right answer.

Now, let me tell you something about Jesus. Jesus was a great teacher. People used to listen to him teach, because they loved to listen to him. When Jesus taught something about God, they knew he was right. They might not like everything that he said, because sometimes he was talking about things that they did wrong, but they knew he was right. They didn't have to check with someone else to see if they agreed with Jesus, because when Jesus spoke it sounded like the power of God. Jesus didn't say that he was right because this was the same thing that someone else said or other people had said. When Jesus spoke, it made people think that he knew the answer better than anyone else ever knew it. Jesus was one of a kind. There was no one else like him. Jesus was the only one and everyone else listened to him. The Bible says that Jesus was the *authority*. That means that what he said started with him and it was right. There was no question that Jesus was right.

That is why I think that in a group of marbles where ten are one color and one is another color, you can pick out the one that is different from all of the rest. Everything else about the marbles is the same. They are all the same size, they are round and they weigh the same. But one is different. Jesus looked the same, but when he spoke, everyone knew he was different. Jesus was the Authority, and when we want to know what God was like we listen to him. Amen.

Traveling Light

Mark 1:29-39

But he replied, "We must go on to other towns as well, and give my message to them too, for that is why I came." (v. 38)

Object: *A man's traveling kit (razor, comb, toothbrush and toothpaste, etc.).*

Good morning, boys and girls. How many of you have ever taken a trip for just one night and then come back home the next day? *(Let them answer.)* Do you take along a lot of suitcases and groceries and things like you do when you take a long vacation? *(Let them answer.)* Of course not. A lot of men have to make trips like that because of the work they do. They don't take a lot of clothes and other things. Many of them only take what I have here in my hand. *(Show them the travel kit.)* That's a pretty small suitcase, isn't it? Do you know what a man takes with him in such a small travel case? *(Let them answer.)* That's right, a toothbrush, toothpaste, razor, comb, and some other things. We call that "traveling light."

Jesus did a lot of traveling. He walked from one town to another visiting with people. There were no buses or trains or cars or airplanes. They could ride on donkeys or some other kind of animal, but most of the time they walked. Jesus had to travel light, and I suppose he took with him only the things that he had to have and nothing else. Why did he visit so many places? Do you know the answer to that question? I'll tell you why. He had a message to share with all of the people about the good things that God did for them and how much God loved everyone. Jesus also showed the love that God had for the people by healing the ones who were sick, and forgiving the people who had sinned. Jesus could have stayed in one place and waited for the people to come to him, but that was not his way. He traveled everywhere that his feet would take him and shared this love that God has for people.

Jesus was a traveler. He traveled light, but he took with him more love than anyone else ever knew there was. You can't carry love in a suitcase. Love is in your heart and the more that you use it the more of it you have to share with others. Jesus didn't need a lot of clothes or furniture to show his love. He needed to give his love to people and to show them that God was like a father to them.

Maybe the next time you see a travel kit or some small suitcase, you will remember all of the traveling that Jesus did and how he shared his love with all the people he met. Amen.

It's Official

Mark 1:40-45

Jesus then told them sternly, "Go and be examined immediately by the Jewish priest. Don't stop to speak to anyone along the way." (v. 43)

Object: *A driver's license.*

Good morning, boys and girls. I want to tell you a little story this morning that I think you will really like. But first you must look at something I brought with me and tell me what it is. *(Take out your driver's license and show them.)* Do you know what this is? *(Let them answer.)* That's right, a driver's license. I suppose you know that you must have one of these to drive a car, don't you? *(Let them answer.)* It doesn't teach you how to drive, but you must have one of these if you are going to drive. It is official, and if you drive a car without a license, you can be arrested and fined a lot of money. It doesn't make any difference how well you drive, or if you don't have an accident. You must have a license.

Now, Jesus knew all about things that were official. Jesus was sure that other people also knew about things that were official. One day Jesus healed a man who had been sick for a long time. It was really a good thing for him to do, and the man was really happy that Jesus had taken care of him. Everyone knew that the man had been sick for a long time and, because of his sickness, he was not able to work or live with his family, for fear that they would also get the same sickness. Once in a great while, someone would get over the sickness, but, before they could go home or take a new job, they would have to go to the temple and have the priest tell them that they were really all right. If the priest did not make it official, it was like it did not happen. It didn't make any difference how good you felt, it had to be done. That's why Jesus told the man to go to the temple to tell the priest, but Jesus also told the man not to tell anyone else.

Jesus had a good reason for asking him to only tell the priest. Jesus knew that if anyone else found out, they would follow *him* so closely and ask him so many questions about who he was, he would get nothing else finished. But the man was so glad and his heart was so filled with joy that, on his way to the temple, he told everyone about the miracle that Jesus had done for him. It was not official, of course, since the priest had not seen him, but the people who saw the man believed that Jesus had done a miracle.

Later the man did make it official, like a driver's license, and the people did follow Jesus everywhere until he could not teach or preach in the town any longer. But this is the story of how Jesus healed one man one day, and what happened when he made it official. Amen.

God is the Only One

Mark 2:1-12

"What? This is blasphemy! Does he think he is God? For only God can fogive sins." (v. 7)

Object: *A Social Security card.*

Good morning, boys and girls. Did you know that only God can forgive sins? *(Let them answer.)* That's right, only God can forgive sins. No one else in the whole world can forgive a sin but God. The word "only" is a pretty big word if it means that there is one person who can do something. I brought along with me this morning a card that belongs only to me. It is called my Social Security card. Your parents and many other people have a Social Security card, but this one is the only one that has this number on it. If I asked everyone here this morning to look at his or her Social Security card, they would see that no one here has my number. Everyone has a different number, and that number belongs only to him or her. No one else can use it. There is only one number for each of us.

God is the only one to forgive sins. You may tell some-one else that you are sorry for what you have done, and they can forgive you for the bad thing that you did to them, but they cannot take away the sin. Only God can erase your sin so that it looks like it has never been done. Some people can fix cars when they are broken, and some people can sew up your clothes when they are torn, but only God can forgive a sin.

Isn't that something? I think it is. It means that when we have done something really wrong and have broken the Ten Commandments, we cannot go to our father or mother or pastor or anyone and ask them to forgive our sins. We can tell them what we did and we will feel better after we have told them, but we cannot have them forgive our sins. There are not any other gods in the world that can do it either. There is just one God and he is in charge of forgiving all of the sins in the whole world. Since everybody sins at one time or another, everyone has to come to the only God and ask his forgiveness. No wonder that God knows us so well. He knows us better than even our father or mother. When we sin, we like to keep it a secret. Sometimes no one else knows what we have done but us, that is, except God. God knows when we have done wrong, and the only way to be forgiven and to feel better is to ask God to forgive us. No wonder God knows us so well.

The next time you see a Social Security card, or when you ask to see your father's or mother's card and you see that they have the only card with that number, I want you to think about God and how he is the only one who can forgive sins. Amen.

Right Way, Wrong Way

Mark 2:23-28

And he said to them, "The sabbath was made for man, not man for the sabbath; so the Son of man is lord of the sabbath." (v. 27)

Object: *Some makeup (if you would like, you may have two girls made up ahead of time. One of them would have on the right amount of makeup and the other would abuse herself with overuse of it.)*

Good morning, boys and girls. Today we are going to do something that I know all the girls know something about and may have even tried once or twice. How many of you know what I mean when I talk about makeup? *(Let them answer.)* Almost all of you know what it is. What are some of the things girls use when they put on their makeup? *(Let them answer.)* That's right, lipstick, powder, eye shadow, and I guess there are a lot of other things that I don't know anything about. Do you think it makes the girls look prettier when they wear these things? *(Let the boys answer.)* If it is used right, it is very nice, but if it is used wrong, it can make a girl look awful. *(Here is the place to use your volunteers, if you have selected them and had them made up in advance.)* There is a right way and a wrong way. Sometimes girls use too much of a good thing and, instead of getting prettier, they are less pretty. The makeup is supposed to help you see better what is already there. When you use too much you take away rather than make better.

The reason I shared this with you is because people often do the same thing with Sunday that girls do with their makeup. People try to make a Sunday such a holy day that they forget why God made it a special day. A long time ago Jesus found people attacking his disciples, because they picked some grain to eat on their day that was like our Sunday. The disciples had not eaten and they were hungry. Jesus told the men who were speaking against him and his disciples that God made that day special for men, and he did not make the men for a special day. Our Sunday is a time to remember what God made for us and all of the wonderful ways in which he did it. But if we fill ourselves with so many ways to remember God that we can't think of what to do next, then we are doing with Sunday what the girls do with their makeup. Too much is worse than none at all. God made Sunday as a day of rest for all of us, and a time to worship God in love and beauty. We should not fill it up with work or with just fun, or with rules that we must break to stay healthy. This is God's world and he made it for us to enjoy and share in love and friendship. Sunday is a time for all of us to remember that, and to thank God for giving to us the world and each other. The next time you see some girls putting on their makeup, I want you to think of how the right amount is important, and how too much is bad, Then you can think of the way we should use Sunday, and how we should fill it with worship and rest and love and fun. The right amount is the right thing. Amen.

On Jesus' Team

Mark 3:20-35

If a kingdom is divided against itself, that kingdom cannot stand. (v. 24)

Object: Fold some paper so that it has two legs on which to stand.

Good morning, boys and girls. Today we are going to talk about how important it is to stick together as Christians. We probably don't think about this very often, but as Jesus said, it is important that we stand up for each other.

Let me show you what I mean. I have with me some stiff paper that we can fold and make legs so that the paper can stand up. We can do this with a lot of pieces if we want to and have them standing up all over the place. But if I take a pair of scissors and cut the paper in half so that it only has one leg on either side, what will happen? *(Let them answer.)* That's right, the paper will fall. You can fold the paper and make two legs again if you want to, but if you divide the paper again the same thing is going to happen. It cannot stand when it is divided. Jesus was not talking about paper when he talked about things dividing. Jesus was talking about good and evil. Evil is not good sometimes and evil at other times, and good is not good sometimes and evil at other times.

The devil is evil all of the time, and the devil is always trying to do bad things to people. Jesus, the Son of God, is always good, and he is always doing good things for people. That is what Jesus was trying to teach the people about him self and the devil.

Some people thought that the things Jesus did, such as healing people with diseases they thought were made by the devil, made Jesus a friend of the devil. They also thought that some of the people whom Jesus made as friends were evil, and that this made Jesus a friend of the devil. But Jesus told them that healing diseases and making good men out of bad men was not the work of a friend of the devil, but, rather, an enemy of the devil. Friends do not work against each other. Friends do not divide, but, rather, they stand together. Jesus said that he was not a friend of the devil, and the devil was not a friend of his.

Jesus wants his friends to stand with him, just as the paper with two legs stands. Jesus also wants us to help divide the world of the devil, like we do when we divide the paper in half. It is good for us to work with Jesus and with the friends of Jesus. When we are sharing our love and our help with people, then we are quickly dividing the world of the devil and not letting him get strong in his struggle with Jesus. Amen.

It Just Grows and Grows

Mark 4:26-34

"It is like a grain of mustard seed, which, when sown upon the ground, is the smallest of all the seeds on earth; yet when it is sown it grows up and becomes the greatest of all shrubs, and puts forth large branches, so that the birds of the air make nests in its shade." (vv. 31-32)

Object: *Some detergent, a dirty glass and a bucket of water.*

Good morning, boys and girls. Today we have a small experiment to try that will teach us something about the Kingdom of God. People like to ask all kinds of questions about the world that God is making for people who believe in him, They want to know where it is and who will be in it. Some people want to know how large it is, and if there will be a good place for them to live in it. The only answers that we have for questions like this are in the Bible. Jesus talked a lot about the Kingdom of God, and when he did he said some things that we can think about. For instance, there were some people who wanted to know how the Kingdom of God would begin and how large it would be.

Jesus told the story about the mustard seed and how, when it was planted, it was the smallest seed that he knew; but when it grew it became such a large plant that the birds made their nests in it. I can't make a mustard seed grow into a large plant today, but I can show you what Jesus was talking about by using something else.

Let's suppose that this powder was the Kingdom of God.

do you see how small each grain of powder is when you take it apart and look at only one grain at a time? *(Let them answer.)* That's pretty small, isn't it? Now, I am going to take just a little bit of this powder and put it in some water. Watch what happens to the powder. *(Stir it up until you have real suds.)* The powder has really turned into something powerful, hasn't it? Let me take this dirty glass and put it into the suds and see what happens. It cleans it in a second. The glass is beautiful.

Well, that is the way the Kingdom of God works on us. God puts just a little bit of his love into this world and shows us what the new world, that he is building, is going to be like. When people like you and me see how wonderful the Kingdom of God is for us, we want to belong and we want all of our friends to know about it, too. It may have started small, with only a couple of people really knowing Jesus and the kind of love that he had for people, but by now the whole world knows about his love and what it can do for people who really need it.

And I can tell you that it really does the job. It cleans us up in a hurry and makes us ready for the Kingdom. Is it going to be big enough for you and me and for all of our friends? It sure is. It is going to be large enough for all of the people who love God and who will love the world that he has built for them. Amen.

Sound Asleep

Mark 4:35-41

But he was in the stern, asleep on the cushion; and they woke him and said to him, "Teacher, do you not care if we perish?" (v. 38)

Object: *A cushion or pillow.*

Good morning, boys and girls. How many of you have ever gone fishing? *(Let them answer.)* Fishing is really fun if you catch some fish, but if you have to just sit and do nothing but wait for the fish to nibble on your line every once in a while, it can be pretty boring. Have you ever been fishing in a boat? *(Let them answer.)* That seems like a lot more fun, doesn't it? Even if you can't catch fish, you can always have a nice ride while you sit in the warm sunshine, and let your hands skim through the cool water.

The disciples and Jesus used to take a lot of boat rides. They didn't have cars or buses, so it was one of the ways that they chose to get from place to place. They often rode in a boat from one side of a lake to the other. This was also a good place for Jesus to take a nap, since he had little time for sleeping when he was around people. They wanted him to heal their sick or teach them about the ways of God. Once in a while, Jesus would tell the disciples that he wanted to go somewhere else and that they should get a boat, so that they could cross over to the other side of the lake.

It was a day like this, that Jesus was sleeping on a cushion at the front of the boat, when a terrible wind storm came up and made great waves. Riding in a boat, with his head upon the cushion, Jesus was sleeping after some very busy days. But the disciples were not asleep. They saw the huge waves and became very much afraid that the boat would turn over in the storm and they would all drown. They knew how tired Jesus was and they hoped that he would wake up on his own, when he felt the boat toss and turn in the storm. But Jesus was so tired and completely unafraid that he never moved. He remained very quiet with his head upon the cushion. Finally, one of the disciples became so afraid that he screamed at Jesus to wake up and do something about the storm before they all drowned. Jesus did wake up, and he looked at the waves which were pounding at the boat and then, with a very quiet voice, he told the waves to calm down. The waves were no more. The lake was calm and the disciples were almost more afraid of his power than they were of the storm, "Just think," they said, "he speaks and even the seas listen to him and obey him." No one had ever seen such power before.

Maybe you have a cushion that you sleep on sometimes. The next time you sleep on it, you can think about the day that Jesus spoke to the sea, and the waves calmed down and became quiet. Will you do that? Good. Amen.

Where the Power Is

Mark 5:21-24a, 35-43

And Jesus, perceiving in himself that power had gone forth from him, immediately turned about in the crowd and said, "Who touched my garments?" (v. 30)

Object: *An electric toaster and some pieces of bread.*

Good morning, boys and girls. Today we are going to work with something that all of you use a lot at home. *(Bring out the toaster and plug it in so that the pieces of bread can be toasting while you are talking.)* How many of you do this once in a while for breakfast? A lot of you. Do you know what is going to happen to those two pieces of bread that I put into this thing? *(Let them answer.)* That's right, they are going to be toasted. Somehow or another, that toaster is going to give off enough power to make regular bread into toast. It doesn't just happen. It takes power from the toaster to make the bread into toast. I don't know if the toaster knows it can give that kind of power, but I know someone who did know whenever he gave away some of his power to another person.

That's right. Jesus was the person who was kind of like my toaster. I remember a story about a woman who had been sick for a long time and was getting weaker and weaker. One day, when she heard that Jesus was coming near to where she lived, she made herself walk to where there was already a crowd. Then when she saw Jesus, she said a quick prayer and touched his clothes. Just like that, Jesus turned around and asked who it was who had touched him and made himself well. Jesus knew that his power had gone out of his body and into the body of someone else. He was glad, but he wanted to know who it was that believed so much in him that he would say a prayer and touch his clothes, knowing that he would be healed.

Now the woman was frightened because she could feel that she was well for the first time in a long time. This is what she thought would happen, but when it did, she was amazed at the power of Jesus. He had made her well. She came over to where he stood and fell down on her knees to tell him the whole story. Jesus saw what a wonderful thing had happened, and he put his hand on her head and told her to go on home and not to worry, for it was her believing that he could heal her that made her well.

Maybe the next time you see a toaster work and watch it use the power to make toast, you will think about the time that Jesus healed a woman when she touched his clothes. He, too, had great power, even the power to make sick people well, and he used it to make people feel closer to God. Amen.

What a Leader!

Mark 6:30-34

As he landed he saw a great throng, and he had compassion on them, because they were like sheep without a shepherd; and he began to teach them many things. (v. 34)

Object: *Some nails and a magnet.*

Good morning, boys and girls. I brought with me this morning something that is a lot of fun to play with when you have nothing else to do. *(Show them the magnet.)* Of course, it is not always used as a toy. Sometimes it is a very valuable tool. How many of you know what this is? *(Let them answer.)* That's right, it is a magnet. Have you ever used one? *(Let them answer.)* Well, let's think about what a magnet does while I show you something else.

(Take out the nails and spread them over the floor.) Have you ever looked at a bunch of nails when they are spread out like this? Can you tell which direction they are heading? *(Let them answer.)* It's kind of a mess, isn't it? The nails should have a leader, something to bring them together. Can you see any nail that could be a leader and bring the rest of the nails together in one place? *(See if they select one of the nails because it is the largest or thickest and then urge that nail to become a leader.)* That was a good choice since it is the biggest nail, but it doesn't seem to be able to bring the nails together. Now, suppose we ask the magnet if it could be a leader of the nails. *(Point the magnet to the nails and begin collecting them.)* That's what I call a leader! Did you see the

way the nails followed our magnet? The nails love the magnet, and they are willing to follow the magnet anywhere. Well, that is the way it is with Jesus and the people. We are like the nails. We are all going in our own way, with no real leader that all of us can follow. Jesus is like the magnet, He is our leader, and we can hardly wait to follow him. When Jesus comes to us and asks us to follow him, then we are ready. We want to go where he goes.

It was the same way when Jesus was walking on the earth. People followed him wherever he went. If he took a boat ride, they ran around the shore so that they would be at the place where he would land when the boat ride was over. That is the way it is today. We still look for Jesus to lead us. We read about him, listen to stories about him, and pray to him, so that he will tell us what to do and when to do it. I hope that you are like one of my nails. I want you to follow him when he calls you, and I want you to know him as your leader. Amen.

Check Inside

Mark 7:1-8, 14-15, 21-23

"There is nothing outside a man which by going into him can defile him; but the things which come out of a man are what defile him." (v. 15)

Object: *A flashlight with some good batteries and some bad batteries.*

Good morning, boys and girls. How many of you have a flashlight at home? Do you use it? *(Let them answer.)* Do you think that your flashlight is working right now, or is not working? *(Let them answer.)* Most of the time when I want to use my flashlight, it does not work. I would like to just beat that flashlight over and over because it won't work. It should work. It looks just great. The switch is fine. The metal looks great, so nice and shiny. It has a bulb in it, and the glass is clean, but I cannot make my flashlight work. Do any of you know what could be wrong with my flashlight? *(Let them answer.)* What do you mean that I should check my batteries? I can't see any batteries. You mean thare are batteries inside of my flashlight? You think that this is what is wrong with my flashlight? That's right. It is something on the inside and not on the outside that is keeping my flashlight from working.

That is like people. Most people think that what is wrong is with all of the things that happen on the outside. They think that the boss is wrong, or their friend is wrong, or they are not making enough money. Some people like to blame the President of the United States for all of their troubles. But

Jesus said that most things that he knew that hurt a man were things that were wrong on the inside of each man or boy or girl. He said that the problem was within us, and not outside of us. Do you think that you cause most of your un-happiness by not being honest, or by picking on a friend or brother or sister? Do you feel unhappy when you talk back to your mother or father? Those are the things that really make us feel bad and keep us from working the way that God wants us to be able to work.

You think that my flashlight will not work because the in-sides are bad. If I change the insides, will that make my flash-light work again? *(Let them answer.)* Will you work better if you get rid of all the meanness or the lies or the trouble that is caused by you on the inside? We call that inside stuff "sin." *(Let them answer,)* Good!

(Open up the flashlight and put in new batteries. Then try it and show them how it works.) Isn't that wonderful? If I fix the insides of the flashlight, it works just fine, the way that it is supposed to. I think we could say the same thing would happen to you and me. If we are good on the inside, then we will work just great on the outside. Maybe you can be fixed to be as good as my flashlight. Amen.

You Can't Hold it Back

Mark 7:31-37

And he charged them to tell no one; but the more he charged them, the more zealously they proclaimed it. (v. 36)

Object: *A bottle of Coke or some carbonated soft drink.*

Good morning, boys and girls. Today I want to tell you about a story of Jesus and how people felt about him. I don't know if you remember reading any stories about Jesus, and how excited the people were when they saw him, but I want to tell you a story about that today.

One day, Jesus healed a man who had never been able to hear or speak before. The people had known this man for a long time, and they were used to him, but they felt kind of sorry for him. Here he was unable to work or talk to the people who loved and cared for him. When they saw Jesus, and they remembered the stories that they had heard about him, they wanted Jesus to heal this man. Well, I know that you know what Jesus wanted to do. He wanted to heal him so that he could speak and hear for the first time. Jesus did exactly that, and the man was so happy, he could hardly wait to tell someone how wonderful God was to send Jesus to him. But he was not the only happy man. Everyone in town was happy. They were so happy that they wanted to tell everyone. Yet because he knew that everyone would not understand, but would think that it was magic or something terrible, he told them not to tell anyone.

Now, I want to break into the story and ask you if you have

ever taken a pop bottle and put your thumb over the opening and then shook it. *(Show them what you mean.)* If you have ever done this or watched someone else do it, you know what will happen. Do you know what will happen? *(Let them answer.)* That's right, it will go all over as soon as you take your thumb or finger away.

That's what happened to the people around Jesus. As long as he was there, it was all right, but as soon as Jesus left, the people went everywhere. They ran as fast as their legs would take them to tell everyone that they knew about the wonderful things that Jesus had done in their town. There was no way to keep them from talking. They ran this way and that way, praising God and telling the world about Jesus.

Like I said, Jesus did not want them to tell, but the more he told them not to, the more they ran and did it.

That was the way it was in just one town. Maybe the next time that you see a bottle of pop. you will remember how excited the people were about the things that Jesus did, and how one day they were so excited that, even though Jesus asked them not to tell, they still did, because they could not keep quiet inside. Amen.

The Most Important Decision

Mark 8:27-35

And he called to him the multitude with his disciples, and said to them, "If any man would come after me, let him deny himself and take up his cross and follow me." (v. 34)

Object: *Some campaign signs that call for "Reagan for President" or "Mondale for President."*

Good morning, boys and girls. Every four years we have an election in our country to decide who is going to be president for the next four years. Two men run for president, and only one of them can win. All of us want one man or the other to be our next president. Would any of you like to be president of our country some day? *(Let them answer.)* That's good. We need people like you who want to be president of our country.

Do you think there are more than two people who want to be president of our country? *(Let them answer.)* I think that there are a lot of people who would like to be president, but only one man can be president. One man is the President of the United States for four years and all of the rest of us will follow him.

Well, it is something like that with Jesus, except that we are not going to elect him. There is only one God. There is only one Jesus. Jesus is our Lord and everyone who wants to follow God must follow him. There is no other choice. We are not going to elect God. But we must all follow him.

Jesus even said that if we want to follow him, we must

first stop trying to be our own boss and give our life to him. That is how we become Christians. We are followers of Jesus, and Jesus comes first. Jesus even comes first before us. We can't do the things that we want and still do the other things that Jesus asks. It doesn't work that way. We have to do the things that Jesus asks first, and then we can do the other things. To be a follower of Jesus, you must put him first and yourself second.

When we elect a president, we agree to follow his leadership for four years. When we agree to be a Christian it means that we agree to follow Jesus for the rest of our lives. It is important to follow a president, but the most important thing that you will ever do is to agree to follow Jesus, for that is the most important decision of your life. Amen.

Give it Away

Mark 8:31-38

For whoever would save his life will lose it; and whoever loses his life for my sake and the gospel's will save it. (v. 35)

Object: *Two bars of soap. One bar should be brand new and the other almost used up.*

Good morning, boys and girls. Today we are going to hear the story about two bars of soap. How many of you use soap? *(Let them answer.)* Very good. Almost everyone uses it. What do you like most about soap? *(Let them answer.)* That's right, it gets you clean.

A bar of soap is a pretty wonderful thing. I suppose you know that the more it is used, the smaller it gets. The better the soap is, the faster it goes away. It isn't like a muscle. The more you use a muscle the bigger it gets. But that is not the way it is with soap.

Take a look at the soap I brought with me this morning. This one bar of soap, we call it Sammy, is always hiding in the drawer. Whenever you need some soap, Sammy hides under a towel or in the corner of the drawer and just prays that you will not see him. He is never used, and he lives all of his life being afraid. Poor Sammy.

But take a look at Sudsy. We call this bar of soap Sudsy because he cannot wait until morning when everyone takes a shower. As soon as you come into the bathroom, he begins to smile and be happy because he knows that he is going to be used for what he was made. When you pick him up, he makes the fluffiest suds in the whole world. Good old Sudsy is glad to know that he is getting smaller and smaller, because he knows that he is being used and making people happy.

Our lives are just like Sammy. Some people are afraid to be a Christian because they think that Jesus will use them for some great job. They are always hiding from God, and trying to save their life to do something for themselves. They stay about the same, they never are used, and they are quite unhappy.

But there are other people who are more like Sudsy. They get up every day looking for another way to serve God. They know that this is the reason that God made them, and they want to serve God in the best way possible. Giving their life to God is what makes them happy and why they enjoy life so much. There are a lot of Sammys who try to keep everything to themselves and are afraid of everything. There are a lot of Sudsys who give their lives to serving God and other people. You have to decide what kind of a person you are going to be. Are you going to be a Sammy? *(Let them answer.)* Are you going to be a Sudsy? *(Let them answer.)* Choose to be a Sudsy and give your life to God. Amen.

"Your Attention, Please!"

Mark 9:2-9

But while he was still speaking these words, a cloud covered them, blotting out the sun, and a voice from the cloud said, "This is my beloved Son. Listen to him." (v. 7)

Object: *A voice coming by microphone from an unseen person (the speaker is visible).*

Good morning, boys and girls. I want you to be very quiet for a moment and just listen very carefully. *(In a booming voice, let someone unseen introduce you with some fanfare over a loudspeaker system.)* Wasn't that something! Did all of you hear that voice? *(Let them answer.)* Where did the sound come from? *(Let them answer.)* From the loud-speaker. Let's listen again and see if we can figure out who is speaking. *(Let the voice repeat what he said the first time.)* Wow! Wow! Wasn't that something? What do you call the thing that just happened? *(Let them answer.)* That is pretty impressive. We call that an introduction. That means that someone is telling you who I am and what I can do. The voice that we don't see but only hear is introducing me to you.

Something like that, only a lot better, happened to three of Jesus' disciples a long time ago. They were on top of a mountain with Jesus when all of a sudden a brilliant cloud passed over the top of them, and a very big voice said, "This is my beloved Son. Listen to him." Do you know whose voice it was in the cloud? *(Let them answer.)* That's right, it was the voice of God the Father. He was introducing his son,

Jesus, as someone to whom they should listen. They thought that Jesus was pretty great before this moment, but after that introduction they knew he was something *very* special.

God the Father introduced Jesus with a voice that came through the cloud, and the disciples never forgot what they heard for as long as they lived.

The next time you hear someone introduced over a microphone as being someone special. I want you to think about the time that Jesus was introduced by God, the Father, to Peter, James, and John as the Son of God. That was the most wonderful introduction that anyone was ever given and the one that everyone remembers the most. God bless you. Amen.

"Me First"

Mark 9:30-37

And he sat down and called the twelve, and he said to them, "If any one would be first, he must be last of all and servant of all." (v. 35)

Object: A human pyramid.

Good morning, boys and girls. How many of you like to be first? *(Let them answer.)* Almost all of us like to be first. I remember when Jesus was walking down the road and listening to his disciples talking about which one was first with him. They all wanted to be the most important person that Jesus had among his followers. Jesus didn't say anything while they were talking, but he listened to them as they each told why they thought that they were the most important person to Jesus. Each one thought that he was first with Jesus.

I need someone to be first. Do I have a volunteer who would like to be first for a little experiment that I am going to do this morning? *(Take the largest child who volunteers to be the first one and then each child after that so that you can build a human pyramid. Hold their hands so that they do not fall or hurt one another.)* Isn't this fun? I wonder how the person who wanted to be first feels now. The first one is on the bottom and is helping to hold every one else up. He is not only the first, but also the hardest worker in the group. He is helping to serve everyone else by being first.

That is the thing that Jesus told his disciples when they finished their walk. He asked all of them who wanted to be first to remember that being first with him meant that they had to be willing to serve everyone else. The person on the bottom of our pile wanted to be first, so he got the chance to hold up the whole group. Being a leader is fun, but it also has tremendous responsibility. You have to help others to be a leader. Jesus needs leaders, but he needs leaders who want to work and do things for others. That is the way it is to be with Jesus.

The disciples thought about that for a long time. Most people want to be first because they like the other people who are already leaders. Most people forget that it took a lot of work to become a leader. If you want to be first, or be a leader, then you must also be ready to serve or help others.

How many of you want to be first now? How many of you would rather be a follower than a leader? That is your decision, but whatever way you want to be with Jesus, he wants you to know that he loves you just as much as he loves the other. Amen.

Room for Differences

Mark 9:38-50

But Jesus said, "Do not forbid him; for no one who does a mighty work in my name will be able soon after to speak evil of me." (v. 39)

Object: *Many different pictures of Jesus.*

Good morning, boys and girls. I have brought with me this morning some pictures of Jesus. I would like you to look at all of them and then choose your favorite one. If we have time I would also like you to tell me why you like one of them more than the other. *(Show the pictures to the children and comment on the differences. The color of his skin, the length of his hair, the kind of clothes he has on, what he is doing, etc. . . .)* Now that every one has had a chance to see the pictures, I want you to tell me which one is your favorite.

I see that all of you have chosen different ones. Some of you like this one, and some of you like this one, and a couple of you even like this one. We each have our choice, and I think that this is good. We don't know what Jesus really looked like, but these are pictures by a certain artist because he believes Jesus looked one way or another. Did you know that all of the pictures were of Jesus? *(Let them answer.)* They are.

Does it make any difference to you if he has blonde hair or black hair, or if his clothes look different in one picture than they do in another? *(Let them answer.)* I hope not. Everyone has a little bit different idea of what Jesus looked like and what he did, That is why we have so many different churches. But Jesus said that the important thing is that everyone follow him, and that they do not speak bad about him. As long as people are doing good because they believe in Jesus, then Jesus said that they should not be stopped. Maybe you wish that everyone thought the way that you think about Jesus. Maybe I wish that everyone would think my way, but Jesus said that we should not get upset about things like that. We should praise God because so many people feel good about Jesus and do good things for others because they believe in him.

People do things and believe things about Jesus that are different than the way that we believe and do things, but there is nothing wrong with that. Remember, as long as they believe and also do good, then they will never speak bad about our God.

Everyone has a different idea of the way Jesus looked, and some people can draw pictures of what they think. That's all right, and we love to see the different ideas. Treat everyone that believes in Jesus with great love and respect and be glad that they love God also. Amen.

Keep it Simple

Mark 10:2-16

Truly I say to you, whoever does not receive the kingdom of God like a child shall not enter it. (v. 15)

Object: *A jar of pickles, mustard, catsup, onion, mayonnaise, lettuce, cheese, tomato, relish and anything else you might put on a hamburger.*

Good morning, boys and girls. Today we are going to talk about keeping things simple. Being simple is the best way, and usually it is the easiest way. I want to prove something to you and to everyone here so you will have to help me.

How many of you like hamburgers? *(Let them answer.)* Everyone likes a good hamburger. Now I want everyone to tell me what you like on your hamburger. First of all, I want you to hold up your hands, and, if you do not like something that I am going to put on your hamburger, then I want you to take your hand down and keep it down. I want you to have only the things on it that you really want on it.

(Now begin by adding cheese, and then catsup, mustard, etc. until you have put down every hand.) Now nobody wants this hamburger. It has all of the good things that I could think of on it, but nobody wants it. We started out with a plain simple hamburger, but by the time we added the cheese, the tomato, the mustard and catsup, the onion, the relish and lettuce and all of the other good things, it became something that no one wanted. I understand this, and I hope that you will understand what I am going to tell you.

Some people like to make God's kingdom a very complicated thing. It is the place of God, where all of us live in peace and love with God. Some people want to make it very hard to get into God's kingdom and make God very hard to live with. They want you to believe everything they say is true. The kingdom is not a complicated place. It is a very simple place.

God's kingdom is like a hamburger without all of the other things. It is so simple that the smallest child knows what it is like to be a part of God's Kingdom. You may not explain it, but it is for all of us. If you keep adding things to it, you find it is a lot like the hamburger I tried to make for you. You don't want it when you put everything on it. That is the way that Jesus felt about the Kingdom of God. It is not complicated. It is so simple that the youngest child can believe in it without any fear.

The next time you sit down and are ready to eat a hamburger, maybe you will remember the time I told you that God's kingdom is like a hamburger without all of the special things on it. Then I hope you remember why I told you that it is better without all of the things than with them. Amen.

Servants are Important

Mark 10:35-45

But whoever would be great among you must be your servant.
(v. 43b)

Object: *A baseball bat.*

Good morning, boys and girls. Today we are going to talk about servants and how they can become great. There aren't many servants today like there were a long time ago. Long ago there were people who worked for other people in their homes and lived where they worked. They waited on tables, took care of the gardens, did the cooking, and washed the clothes. Today there are not many people who have servants like that, and so it is hard for us to understand what a servant really does.

Jesus said that a man must be a servant to other men if he is going to be great. That was a new teaching. Most people thought that the great man was the person for whom the servant worked, doing the things that we talked about. But that is not the way Jesus thought about a servant. Jesus felt that it was great when you could do something to make life better for someone else, like a servant did.

Let's use an example. Have you ever tried to hit a ball with your arm? That would hurt, wouldn't it? I mean, suppose someone pitched you a fast ball and you swung with your arm and hit it. Boy, that would hurt. But, let's suppose you have a servant called a bat. This bat is your very favorite bat, because when you swing it and hit the ball, it feels good. That ball seems to go farther and people think that you are a good batter when you hit with this bat. The bat is your servant, and you are proud of that bat. You take good care of the bat, too. You never leave it out in the rain, and you take it with you whenever you want to have fun or play a good game. Your servant, the bat is made of wood and cannot talk, but it sure can hit a baseball. I think you would like that bat for a long time.

That is the way that Jesus thought about people. There were some people who thought that they were too good to work or do anything for anyone else. They needed servants to do everything. These people did not know how to do much at all. As a matter of fact, they could do nothing without a servant. Jesus thought that this was kind of silly. The real people are the ones who can do things, and they enjoy life much more than the people who just wait to have things done for them.

A Christian is a servant of God. He does things. He is also a servant to other men, and is always looking for things to do to make life better. The next time you pick up your favorite bat, I want you yo think of it as a servant, and thank your bat for making the game so much fun for you to play. Then you will know also how much fun you can make life for others. Amen.

No More Begging

Mark 10:46-52

And they came to Jericho; and as he was leaving Jericho with his disciples and a great multitude, Bartimaeus, a blind beggar, the son of Timaeus, was sitting by the roadside. (v. 46)

Object: *A tin cup.*

Good morning, boys and girls. How many of you have ever begged for something? *(Let them answer.)* What did you beg for? *(Let them answer.)* Whom did you beg? *(Let them answer.)* What would you do if you had to beg for the food that you ate everyday, or for a place to sleep at night? Can you imagine what it would be like to get up every morning and know that you were going to have to beg that day, just so that you could live until the next day? Can you imagine how it would be if you had to beg every day, just so you would have something to eat, wear, or a place to sleep? It sounds awful, doesn't it?

A long time ago there was a blind man by the name of Bartimaeus who was like a lot of other blind men. They could not work on the farms or anywhere, so they had to beg to live. *(Show them the tin cup.)* Everyday they would sit at a busy street corner or in front of a busy building like the temple and beg a couple of pennies from the people who came by. It was not a very good life, but it was the only way they had to live.

It was on a day like this that Jesus was coming with his disciples out of the city called Jericho. Bartimaeus, the blind beggar, was sitting by the road with his tin cup begging all of the people who came by. He could not believe how lucky he was to be there when Jesus was coming, and he yelled as loud as he could for Jesus to stop to see him. The people who were close by told him to be quiet and to stop making such a noise. They were embarrassed by the sound that this blind man was making. But Bartimaeus had heard about Jesus and all of the wonderful things that he did, and he wanted Jesus to heal him. He called louder than even before for Jesus to come near him. This time Jesus heard him and came looking for him. Now the people talked differently. They too wanted to see what Jesus would do with the blind man, and so they told him to stand up and begin walking toward Jesus. Bartimaeus did just that and when Jesus saw him, he asked him what he could do for him. Bartimaeus could hardly speak. There he was, standing in front of Jesus with his cup in his hand, trying to speak. Bartimaeus did not want some pennies. Bartimaeus wanted to see, and he asked Jesus to give him back his sight, so that he could work like the other men. Jesus looked at the cup and then at Bartimaeus and told him to open his eyes and walk home. Because Bartimaeus believed that Jesus could heal him, Jesus did heal him, and he was well for ever. Never again would Bartimaeus have to beg with his cup. He would never forget the day that Jesus gave him back his sight. Bartimaeus believed in Jesus forever and so did everyone else who watched what happened that day. Amen.

Roll Out the Red Carpet

Mark 11:1-10

And many spread their garments on the road, and others spread leafy branches which they had cut from the fields. (v. 8)

Object: *Some red carpet; if possible, small pieces of red carpet to hand out.*

Good morning, boys and girls. How many of you have heard people say: "They rolled out the red carpet for him"? *(Let them answer.)* Do you know what rolling out the red carpet means? *(Let them answer.)* It means that you are giving an important person some very special treatment. When the President of the United States goes somewhere to speak, they roll out the red carpet. If the King or Queen of England visits another country, they roll out the red carpet. Sometimes we roll out the red carpet for great writers, musicians, or actors. We roll out the red carpet when someone very important to us visits us and we want them to know how much we think of them.

The reason I am telling you about the red carpet treatment is because the people of Jerusalem gave Jesus the red carpet treatment many years ago. Perhaps you remember the day when Jesus told his disciples to borrow a donkey that had never been ridden before. They borrowed the donkey and brought it to Jesus. Then Jesus did something that he had never done before. He got on the donkey and rode it into Jerusalem as though he were in a great parade. The only thing about this parade was that Jesus was the only person in it.

All the people stared at him at first, and then they began to let out great shouts of praise. "Hosanna! Hosanna!" they cried, which meant, "Blessed is he who comes in the name of the Lord!" And while they were singing and crying out these words, they were taking off their coats and laying them in the street. Others began to cut branches from the trees that had long soft leaves, and laid them in the street also. It was like a carpet, a red carpet, and they meant it to be so. They wanted Jesus to know that he was their King. They wanted to tell him that they believed in what he taught about God the Father. The disciples could hardly believe what they were seeing. It was the best thing that had ever happened to them. Here they were following Jesus and people were treating him like a King. It was great, just great, and they knew that he deserved it. This day people cut palm branches and then spread them on the ground like a carpet for Jesus to ride on.

The next time that you see or hear someone talk about rolling out the red carpet, you will know what they mean. You will also remember the day that the people of Jerusalem treated Jesus like a King. Amen.

It's Not Far Away

Mark 12:28-34

And when Jesus saw that he answered wisely, he said to him, "You are not far from the kingdom of God." And after that no one dared to ask him any question. (v. 34)

Object: *A periscope or binoculars.*

Good morning, boys and girls. How far away do you think the Kingdom of God is today? If you had to give someone directions to get to the Kingdom of God, I wonder how you would tell them to go. Suppose that I gave you this periscope (or these binoculars) and I asked you to show me where the Kingdom of God is, do you think that you could show me? *(Let them answer.)* I wonder if anyone would like to try? None of you think that you could show me where the Kingdom of God is with binoculars or a periscope. How would you show me the way so that I could get in to the Kingdom if I wanted to? *(Let them answer.)*

A lot of people would like to know, and a lot of people have been asking that question for a long time. One man asked Jesus the question in a little different way, and Jesus told him that he was not far from the Kingdom of God. Let me tell you about it.

The Kingdom of God is really not far away. As a matter of fact, you could be in it right now. The Kingdom of God is a place where people love God with all of their hearts and minds. It is also a place where they love other people just as much as they love themselves. That is the Kingdom of God.

It is also where it is if you are looking for it. That means that if you love God with all of your heart, and other people like yourself, then you are in the Kingdom now. The person standing right next to you who does not love God that much, or others as much as themselves, would not be in it. There is going to be more to the Kingdom of God than that, but if you do those things, then you are already a part of God's Kingdom. It is a good feeling, isn't it? You don't have to hunt it. You don't need a map or a pair of binoculars. All you need to do is love God with all of your heart, and other people as much as you love yourself, and you are in.

When the man asked Jesus where the Kingdom of God was and he told them the answer, the man was thrilled. He had worried and looked for God's Kingdom for years and had never found it. Jesus answered his question in a moment, and the man knew that he had the right answer. Love God, love your neighbor, and you are in the Kingdom of God. There is a lot more to come and it gets even better. But for now you will be filled with love and there is nothing that feels better than love. God bless you. Amen.

A Great Day

Mark 16:1-8

And looking up, they saw that the stone was rolled back; for it was very large. (v. 4)

Object: *The largest round stone that you can bring to church and a number of smaller stones that you can pass out to the children.*

Good morning, boys and girls. Do you know that Jesus came back to life from the dead? He promised us that the same thing was going to happen to every one of us who believe that this is God's plan and that Jesus made it possible.

That was quite a day. It did not begin for most people like days usually do. If you know there is going to be a big day tomorrow, you can hardly sleep, you are so excited. You think of all the good things that are going to happen to you, and how you are going to love every minute of it, and you can hardly wait. But, that isn't the way it was for the people who loved Jesus on the day before the first Easter. They cried the most that they had ever cried. Jesus was dead and buried in a cave called the tomb. There was a big rock or stone that covered the door into the tomb. Tht stone was so big and so heavy that one person could not move it. Do you know how heavy a stone is? *(Show them your biggest stone.)* See how heavy this stone is. Can you imagine lifting or moving a stone that was bigger than a door? That's a pretty big stone. It took a lot of men to roll it into the place where it was guarding the door into the tomb. Usually once the stone was put in that place, it was never moved again. It just stayed there.

Some of the women who had been followers of Jesus wanted to do the right thing for a person who had died. Jesus had died late on Friday and the law said that you could not do kind things for the dead after sundown on Friday. And you were not allowed to do anything on Saturday. That is the way that it was then and still is in some parts of the world today. They just had time to put Jesus in the tomb and close it up and that was all. The women decided that they wanted to do something better for Jesus, and so they began to walk toward the place where Jesus had been buried. While they were walking, they talked about the big stone in front of the door, and how they hoped that some of the men or soldiers would be there to help them move it out of the way. That big stone was really on their minds. But when they got to the tomb, they were shocked and surprised. The stone had been moved, and it had not been moved by men or soldiers. There was an angel there who spoke with them and told them that Jesus was no longer in the tomb. He was alive and no longer dead. The angel told them to go and tell the disciples. What a day! Now, they were as happy as they once were sad.

I have a stone for each of you to take home. It is not large, and certainly not as big as the one that stood in front of the tomb. I want you to have it so that you will remember how the big stone was moved by God and how Jesus came back from the dead. Amen.

Extra Special

Luke 1:39-45

And she exclaimed with a loud cry, "Blessed are you among women, and blessed is the fruit of your womb!" (v. 42)

Object: *Some books and a Bible.*

Good morning, boys and girls. I brought along some books with me this morning to help me tell you a story about Mary, the mother of Jesus. I think you will learn something special about her today, and maybe you will also learn something about books. I have this whole box of books I want to show you. I want to see what you think of them. *(Begin to take out the books one at a time.)* I would like to find a really special book to read, and I wonder if you might help help me choose it. There should be a really special book in all of these books. Of course they are all alike in some ways. They all have a cover and a lot of pages. They have words printed on the pages and most of the pages have numbers. Some of the books are longer and the size of the words are different, but they almost all look somewhat alike. Have you noticed any special book among all of the books? *(Let them answer.)* If you have not come to the Bible yet, then ask the question again when they have seen the Bible.) You think the Bible is special. Is it different from the other books? It looks the same. What do you think makes it different? *(Let them answer.)* You're right. God makes that book special.

I think I can show you that God did the same thing with Mary. She was a woman like almost all of the other women.

She looked like them. She walked like them, and she ate like them. Mary probably talked like most of the women. But one day God chose her among all of the women, and had her give birth to the baby Jesus. That made her special. Even before then, one of her relatives named Elizabeth knew that there was something special about Mary, and she told her so. The thing that made Mary special was the baby that God gave her as a special gift to the whole world.

The Bible is different from all other books because of God, and so is Mary special among all mothers because of what God did with her. You may see pictures of Mary or hear stories about her, but I can tell you that she was special among all of the mothers because God chose her to be the mother of Jesus.

Maybe the next time you take a look at a book, you will remember that there is a special book called the Bible. You may also remember then that God chose a special woman by the name of Mary to be the mother of Jesus. Amen.

Making Our Love Increase

Luke 1:46-55

And Mary said, "My soul magnifies the Lord." (v. 46)

Object: *A magnifying glass.*

Good morning, boys and girls. Imagine what it would be like to make yourself as big as you wanted to be with a magic wand, or a special word. How big would you like to be? *(Let them answer.)* That's big. There is something about being big that is exciting. We can hardly wait until we grow up to be as big as our fathers and mothers. To be able to grow tall is wonderful. It's great to grow smart and strong. But the Bible is always telling us that it is even greater to grow another way. I want to talk to you about the way this morning.

Mary, the mother of Jesus, was a true believer in God all of her life. Even when she was a child, she knew that God was something very special to her. I am sure that she prayed and worshiped God every day. But when she was told by God that she was going to have a child, and that the child was going to be special because it was going to be God's son, then she believed even more.

Mary talked about her soul being magnified. How many of you have a magnifying glass? Do you know what a magnifying glass does? *(Let them answer.)* Right, it makes everything look larger and easier to read or see. Mary said that her soul was magnified. It was larger than before. Not only was it larger, but her love for God and the wonderful things that he was able to do was also larger for everyone else to see.

Mary could not stop talking or praising God for the wonderful things that had happened to her.

I wish that we could magnify all of our souls. All of us know something about God, and we think that he is great for the things that he has done for us, but how do we show it? Do we sing songs about God with glad hearts and joyful voices? Do we thank God in prayer and tell others how wonderful God is to share his world with us? Do we thank him for all of the good things that are in the world? That is what we call magnifying the Lord, to make God easy to see for everyone. Let your friends and neighbors know that you know how good God is to you.

When you see a magnifying glass I want you to remember Mary, the mother of Jesus, and how happy she was to be able to serve God. When you think about how glad Mary was, then think about how glad you are to know God and share God's love in the same world with others. Amen.

"I'm Sorry"

Luke 3:1-6

And he went into all the region about the Jordan, preaching a baptism of repentance for the forgiveness of sins. (v. 3)

Object: *A big paddle that you can use for spanking.*

Good morning, boys and girls. How many of you have ever done something that you feel really bad about? *(Let them answer.)* Are you sorry? *(Let them answer.)* Would you like to say that you are so sorry that you will never do it again? *(Let them answer.)* Have you ever done something so bad that you knew when you did it you would be spanked by your mom or dad if they found out about it? *(Let them answer.)*

I brought along something to show you. I am ready to spank anyone with this paddle who thinks they should be spanked for something or many things that they have done and have never been caught. How many of you think this is a good idea? You can stop worrying. This is it. I will give you one big spanking, and we will tell your folks that this one was the one in place of all the little ones that you should have had. Then we can start all over. How many of you think that this is a good idea? If you like, you can line up here and I will give the spankings to you one at a time.

That sounds pretty rough, doesn't it? It is a rough way. I told you this because there is a better way. The real reason I showed you this paddle is because there once was a man named John the Baptizer who preached in Israel before Jesus preached. He just hated all of the things that he saw men do and say. They wanted everyone to think that they were men of God but they did such sneaky things. They only did something good if if looked good, so other men would talk about them and praise them. They liked to praise themselves and would do it when the other men did not praise them enough. John the Baptizer called them snakes, and other names because they were really sneaky. He called them snakes to their faces. Their sins were great, really great. How would a man who tried to fool God as much as he tried to fool people be forgiven? Should John the Baptizer give that man a spanking with a large paddle? One big spanking for all of their sins? That might be one way, but he knew that God had a different way and he told them about it. He said that God doesn't give spankings. He doesn't even believe in spanking. God believes in forgiving rather than spanking. Here is God's plan according to John. If you are really sorry you will have yourself baptized. That showed John how sorry you really were for your sins. To John, that showed you really meant it, and you wanted to be on God's side, and not just on your own side.

Maybe the next time you see a paddle you will think about how God wants you to feel sorry for your sins, but that he has a better way of doing it. It is called baptism and it is a sign of your repentance. Amen.

The Most Important Part

Luke 3:7-18

John answered them all, "I baptize you with water; but he who is mightier than I is coming, the thong of whose sandals I am not worthy to untie; he will baptize you with the Holy Spirit and with fire." (v. 16)

Object: *A soup pan, some water to pour into the pan and soup ingredients to be mixed with the water.*

Good morning, boys and girls. How many of you like soup? *(Let them answer.)* Almost everybody likes soup. On a cold day soup tastes so good that I can hardly wait to eat it after I smell it cooking on the stove. Do you know what it takes to make soup? *(Let them answer.)* That's right, it takes water and other things. Suppose you were going to make tomato soup. It would take water and tomatoes. If you were going to make chicken soup with noodles, it would take water, chicken, and noodles. That sounds simple, doesn't it? I think so.

I want you to remember what we said about the soup, but now I want to tell you about something else. There were two men that lived a long time ago. One was Jesus and the other was John the Baptizer. Now we all know about how important Jesus is to all of us, but I wonder if we know much about the importance of John the Baptizer. I like to think about Jesus and John, like I think about soup. What is the most important part of the soup? *(Let them answer.)* The most important part is the good things you put in it. The chicken or the noodles or the tomatoes are the most important. I think we all agree to that statement. But you need water to start with and I like to think that John the Baptizer is like the water. We start with John the Baptizer, because he is the one who introduced Jesus as the Savior. You would not want soup that was made of water, but you would not want much soup without the water. John the Baptizer knew who was most important. He told everyone that Jesus was so important that he felt funny about even tying the laces on Jesus' sandals. John knew that Jesus was very important. Jesus knew that he needed men like John, and he said so many times. John was like the water that you need to make the soup, but it is not as important as the things you put in it to make the kind of soup you want.

Maybe the next time you see a can of soup or smell the soup cooking on your stove, you will remember how important we said the ingredients were that made a certain kind of soup. I hope you will also remember that while the water was not important, it really helps to make the soup. I hope you will remember that Jesus is the most important, but John the Baptizer was a great help to Jesus. That's something for everyone to remember. Amen.

He Will Take Care of Us

Luke 21:10-19

But not a hair of your head will perish! For if you stand firm, you will win your souls. (vv. 18-19)

Object: *Some different kinds of hair; like blond, brown, black, red.*

Good morning, boys and girls. How many of you have ever been afraid? Good, we have all been afraid at some time or another. Have you ever been so afraid that you felt like running away? *(Let them answer.)* I know what that feels like also. You think that if you run fast enough, you will be able to get away from whatever the bad thing is that is making you feel afraid. Let me ask you one more question. Have you ever been afraid of something that you thought might make you die? *(Let them answer.)* I guess that is what most people are most afraid of no matter how old they are.

Jesus knew what it was like to be afraid. People tried to frighten him all the time. Many people who stayed with him were afraid, and sometimes they were so afraid that they thought they were going to die. There was one big difference between Jesus and other people. Jesus knew that no matter what people said or did to him, there was nothing to worry about. Jesus knew that God was with him and would always be with him if he lived or died. Jesus wanted everyone else to know what he knew, so he would tell people that they had nothing to worry about.

Jesus said that, no matter what someone tried to do to you, if you trusted in God he would protect you so well that you would not even lose a hair on your head.

Have you ever looked at the hairs on your head? I brought some hair with me today so that we could take a look at it. Do you think you would miss one of these hairs if you lost it? *(Show them the hair.)* Do you think you would miss ten hairs or even 100 hairs on your head? You must have 10,000 hairs. Do you think that you would miss 100 hairs? I don't think so, but God says that he won't let you lose one. He is so careful for you, that Jesus says God is going to protect you right into heaven, and he will not let anyone take away even one hair from you. That means that no matter what happens to you here on earth, God will keep you perfect in heaven. You may have a bad time on earth following Jesus and sticking up for him, but Jesus says that the fellow who stays with Jesus and God his Father on earth will have everything in heaven.

No one else can promise you something like this. Only God can tell you that he will take such good care of you that when you come to heaven he will make you perfect. Jesus is asking us to stick up for him on earth and promises us that everything will be great in heaven. Amen.

Jesus is Coming

Luke 21:25-36

So also, when you see these things taking place, you know that the kingdom of God is near. (v. 31)

Object: *Some Christmas tree ornaments.*

Good morning, boys and girls. I brought along some things to help you to remember a time that is kind of easy to forget. *(Take out the ornaments.)* Do you know what these things are? *(Let them answer.)* What do they remind you of? *(Let them answer.)* Christmas. What is Christmas? *(Let them answer.)* When you see an ornament, and it reminds you of Christmas, do you think of Jesus' birthday first? That is what Christmas is really about, isn't it? That is the day that we celebrate the birthday of Jesus and we do it in a lot of ways. We go to church, we spend the day with our families, and we exchange gifts, to remember the great gift that God gave to us, when he sent Jesus into the world.

I wonder if you know that Jesus is coming again. He is. I don't know when, but the Bible tells us that we can count on it. Jesus will come again and live here with us on earth. The Bible says that when certain things happen, like it says are going to happen, and they all happen together, then Jesus is going to come back. This isn't something I made up, because Jesus is the one who said it. You can have your mothers and fathers read it to you in the Bible or let them tell you about it. Some of the things that Jesus told us are like warnings. We will want to be sure that we are alert and sharp, so that we will know that the things that are happening are signs of Jesus coming. We want Jesus to come back again, and the sooner the better. When Jesus comes back, it will be the beginning of the time that God has promised all of us. We will then be part of God's world and all of us will live forever. It is hard for us to know how God is going to do everything, and we can't even understand it all. But then, we don't know how God does a lot of things now, but he does them. When Jesus does come back, we want to be sure that we are ready for him. We want to show him how much we love him and how much we have wanted him to come back and be with us.

Today we have ornaments to remind us of Christmas. Just like ornaments tell of Christmas coming, so there will be signs from God telling us of the coming of Jesus. Pray to God and ask him to send Jesus and to make sure that your love will know him when he comes. Amen.

A Heap of Blessings

John 1:1-18

We have all benefited from the rich blessings he brought to us, blessing upon blessing heaped upon us! (v. 16)

Object: *A lot of girl's clothing.*

Good morning, boys and girls. Today we are going to kid the girls, and while we are doing it, we will hope to learn something great about the way that God cares for us.

Have you ever heard a girl say, "I don't have a thing to wear?" Girls say that all of the time. Your mother says it, your sister says it, your grandmother and aunt say it, and all of their girlfriends say it. It is just something that girls say. You know what the terrible part of it is is that they mean it. They really believe that they don't have a nice dress, or sweater or skirt to wear. It is like someone came into the house and just took all of their clothes.

I know a girl who says this and I want to show you what kind of clothes this girl has. *(Begin to have as many clothes, girl clothes, as possible carried out to you and take them one at a time for a while and just pile them up.)* Look at this pile of clothes. There is a real heap of clothes! Clothes upon clothes until we can say that there is a heap of clothes! Now, how does this heap of clothes teach us something about God? I'll tell you how. Boys and girls ask each other, "What has God done for me lately?" God sends us his blessings, one after the other every day of our lives, but we have so many that we think we don't have any. God sends us sunshine and rain when we need it. He makes food to grow and gives us material to build our houses. God even gives us the things that it takes to make the clothes that we don't think we have.

God just blesses us and blesses us, until we have a heap of blessings. We have so many blessings that we don't know what to do with all of them. We can't use them fast enough and, before we have used the blessings that God has given us, he has given us some more.

God gave us the love that we have to share with others. God gave us the forgiveness that we have to forgive others. God also gave us the blessings that we have to bless others.

You have a heap of blessings just like the girl I know who has a heap of clothes. But most of us don't know what our blessings are, so we think that we have none. Remember how much God gives you and how much you have, and you will want to share it with others. Also, remember that there is more and more to come from God, and the faster you use your blessings the more God will have to give you. Amen.

"The Church Store"

John 2:13-22

And he told those who sold pigeons, "Take these things away; you shall not make my Father's house a house of trade." (v. 16)

Object: *Different items that you would find in a department store with a sign that says, "THE CHURCH STORE."*

Good morning, boys and girls. How many of you went shopping this weekend with either your mom or dad? *(Let them answer.)* Did you buy a lot of things? *(Let them answer.)* It's kind of fun to go to the store and buy the things that you need at home, isn't it? Sometimes, I think that maybe our church should have a store. Would you like to come to church and buy your clothes and shoes? How about your radios and TVs? Don't you think that our church would make a wonderful store? It's big enough and just think, you could come to church and do your shopping on the same day. I can just see it now. *(Take out the sign.)* THE CHURCH STORE. We could hang our sign out front and invite all of the people to come inside and buy the things that they needed. We might even start a grocery in the Sunday School. Does that sound like a good idea to you? It doesn't! Can anybody tell me why our church would not make a good store. *(Let them answer.)*

I have one very good reason why it would not make a good store. Did you know that Jesus told some people once that they should not make the House of God into a store? It's the truth. He told some people that were selling pigeons, cows, goats, and sheep, that the House of God is for prayer, not for selling things like the animals that we just talked about.

A church is not a store. A church is a place of worship and study. There are other places to sell furniture or clothes or groceries. We don't want to do our shopping in church. When you come in the church, you are supposed to be ready for prayer and to sing praise to God. Jesus does not expect you to go shopping and pray out loud in the store, or to sing a hymn while you are picking out the kind of potatoes that you like for dinner. You don't do that in the store and you are not supposed to do your shopping in church.

Jesus called the church "A House of Prayer." That is a good name for every church. It is a better name than the "Church Store." Maybe the next time you go shopping with your mom and dad, you will remember what we talked about this morning. Then you can be thankful that we have stores in which to shop and churches in which to pray and sing songs to God. Amen.

Brand New Lives

John 3:1-17

Do not marvel that I said to you, "You must be born anew." (v. 7)

Object: *Some ID bracelets from a hospital maternity section.*

Good morning, boys and girls. Today we are going to look at something that almost all of you wore at one time, but at a time that not one of you remembers. *(Bring out the ID bracelets.)* How many of you remember wearing a bracelet like this? *(Let them hold up their hands.)* Do you know where I got these bracelets? *(Let them answer.)* I picked these up at the hospital. There is a place in almost every hospital that is special and is saved for mothers and their babies. How many of you were born in a hospital? *(Let them answer.)* Almost every one of you was born there, and when you were born, the nurse put one of these bracelets on your arm with your mother's name written on it. It may say "baby Smith" or "baby Clark" or whatever your name is. That way, when they put you in the nursery, they know who belongs to you and whom you belong to. That is just one of the things that happens when you are born into this world, but it is an important thing. We all like to know that we belong to our mothers and fathers, and it is important to them that they belong to us. That is our first birth.

Jesus talked about another birth that is even more important. It is called by Jesus, being "born anew." It means that, in addition to having earthly parents, our mothers and fathers, we also have another father who loves us even more than our own father. This father is called our heavenly Father, or God. God loves us in the same way that our father does here on earth, only more so. God the Father will care for us forever, even after we grow old and die and live again. Being born anew like Jesus talked about happens when we become part of God's family. It may happen to us when we are still very tiny children, or it may not happen until we are much older. Jesus knew how important it was to be born the first time and none of us will ever forget the way he was born, but Jesus also knew that being born the second time was even more important for each of us. You can't be born the second time like you were the first time, and Jesus never thought that you would be. The first time you lived in your mother's tummy until just the right time for you to be born. The second time that you are born is also the right time and it may happen soon or much later. But it is the time that God and you become like a father and one of his children. All of us want very much to know how much God loves us and cares for us, and I hope you will be reminded of God's love whenever you see or hear of a child who is born and wears one of these bracelets. Being one of God's children is even greater than being a child of your father and mother, and we all know how wonderful it is to have parents like we have today. Amen.

Darkness and Light

John 3:14-21

For everyone who does evil hates the light, and does not come to the light, lest his deeds should be exposed. (v. 20)

Object:*A burglar's mask and a flashlight.*

Good morning, boys and girls. How many of you have ever seen a robbery on TV? It sounds kind of exciting, doesn't it? *(Let them answer.)* The burglar knows that he is wrong, doesn't he? *(Let them answer.)* He sure does. He doesn't want anyone to know that it is he who is making the robbery. Some robbers even wear masks to hide their faces so that no one will recognize them. *(Put on the mask.)* But most of all, they like to do their robbing at night. *(Take out the flashlight.)* They want the least amount of light that they can have. The light of day is no good for people who do wrong and evil things. If they robbed in the daytime, then people would see them and remember a lot more about them than if they rob at night. Evil people like the night where they can hide the bad things that they do.

Jesus knew this and told us so a long time ago. He told us how people who did wrong like to do it at night. He also told us that people who like to do good can do it in the daytime where everyone can see it. You don't have to be sneaky when you are doing something good. You can do it in the sunshine or without the sunshine. You don't have to wear a mask or carry a flashlight. If you want to help someone who needs help, you can do it at anytime you would like to, and no one will think anything but good about it.

It is too bad that people want to rob or do bad things. Some people don't know how to do good things, so they keep right on doing the bad. But you and I have a chance to show the bad how to do good things. If we want to teach someone that doing bad things are wrong, we must not do something bad to them. We should do it the right way, and do it the right way over and over again. People do not always change the first time they see something done right. Sometimes we have to do it God's way time and time again before we see how much better it is to be able to live in the light and not in the darkness.

I hope that you never see a robber. I hope that you never have to be afraid of the dark. But the next time you see a story on TV about a robber, doing his robbing at night, I want you to think about the ways God says that we should act, and how we can help the evil people in this world by doing good. That is the way of God and the way for you and me. Amen.

The Very Last Day

John 6:41-51

No one can come to me unless the Father who sent me draws him; and I will raise him up the last day. (v. 44)

Object: A nickel, a piece of paper, and a calendar with the 31st of December circled.

Good morning, boys and girls. I brought some things this morning that will help me tell you about one of the teachings of Jesus. I hope it will help you remember something very important. The first thing I brought is a nickel. It is not like any other nickel that I have ever had. It is a very special nickel because it is my last nickel. There are no other nickels, and I will not have any more nickels because this is my last one. That makes it a very important nickel, doesn't it? I will want to choose very carefully the thing I spend my last nickel on, won't I?

I also brought along the last piece of paper from my tablet. I will want to be more careful what I choose to write on this last piece of paper. I won't want to scribble or tear it since there is not another one to use.

Here is something else that is the last. *(Hold up the calendar and turn to December.)* Do you see the number 31? *(Let them answer.)* That is the last day of the year. There will never be another December 31, [insert correct year]. It is the last one, and it is a very important day and we should use it very carefully.

Last things can be very important things. Jesus spoke

about a last thing. He talked about the last day. The last day is not the last day of the week or the year. The last day that Jesus spoke about was the last day of the world, and he knew that this would be a most important day, maybe the most important day that there ever was.

When Jesus talked about the last day, he talked about how all of us who believe in God and his love, will be taken up from the earth to live with the Father in heaven, and with Jesus himself. He is making that place where we will live the most wonderful place there ever was, and some place that all of us will want to live someday. The last is not bad, but it is very important.

Jesus says that we will come to heaven on the invitation of God the Father. God the Father is going to invite us to heaven, and Jesus will then raise us up from the grave if we have died, or off the earth if we are still living. We will not have to be living like we are today to go to be with Jesus. He will find us wherever we are and bring us to him.

So, the next time you have the last of something, remember that the last is not always sad or bad. Sometimes the last is the very best, and the last day of the world will be the best day for all who love Jesus. Amen.

Food From Heaven

John 6:24-35

Jesus said to them, "I am the bread of life; he who comes to me shall not hunger, and he who believes in me shall never thirst." (v. 35)

Object: *Some bread and water.*

Good morning, boys and girls. Is anyone hungry? *(Let them answer.)* Is anyone thirsty? *(Let them answer.)* Would you like some bread and water? *(Pass out bread and water to the hungry and thirsty ones.)* Do you feel a lot better now that you have had something to eat and drink? *(Let them answer.)* That's good because we would never want anyone to leave church feeling hungry or thirsty. It takes food to keep us alive and healthy, doesn't it? *(Let them answer.)* All of us need to eat and drink if we want to be able to walk, think, or do almost anything. If we don't eat or drink then we will die.

There is another kind of food that we need to live forever. This food is not something that we can taste or feel, like the bread and water that I gave to you a few minutes ago. This food is different. It is more important than the kind that we have at home every day. This kind of food is called faith. Can you say the word faith? *(Let them say "faith.")* It's a very important word because it means that you believe in Jesus. Jesus called himself the "bread of life." He meant that if people believed in him as much as they believed in the food that they ate every day, they could live forever. Eating our kind of bread and drinking our kind of water means that we will live only until we grow old, and then we will die. Bread and water cannot keep us alive forever. But believing in Jesus will let us live with God even after we die. That is a very important difference and one that all of us need to learn.

Jesus said that faith is more important than bread or water. When you and I listen to what Jesus teaches and then do it, we are having faith in Jesus. We can't see Jesus, so we must believe that what the Bible tells us about him is true. That is faith.

Now we all know that we must eat our food to stay strong and healthy so that we can grow old. You believe this, and I believe this, and it is true. The same thing is true about believing in Jesus. We must learn to trust what Jesus teaches us now, so that we will have the faith to live forever. Remember that Jesus called himself the Bread of Life because he wanted us to know that, when we take him into our lives, like we take bread into our bodies, we will live with him forever. Amen.

Living Forever

John 6:51-58

"I am the living bread which came down from heaven; if any one eats of this bread, he will live forever; and the bread which I shall give for the life of the world is my flesh." (v. 51)

Object: *A ruler, a ball of string, a calendar.*

Good morning, boys and girls. How long is forever? *(Let them answer.)* Have you ever heard me talk about living forever? *(Let them answer.)* I always talk about living forever. I suppose that every pastor talks about those words more than any other words. But what is forever?

Some things we know about, like: how long some things are or how long they will last. I have a ruler and I know that this ruler is twelve inches long. It isn't thirteen inches or twenty inches long, but twelve inches long. Here is a ball of string. If I stretch it out as far as it will go, I know that it is as long as this church, but not much longer. I also have a calendar. This calendar tells me how many days there are in a year. If you know what day your birthday is on, I can tell you when you are going to change your age. This year you may be seven years old, but on your next birthday, you are going to be eight years old, and you can never be seven again. None of these things then last forever. A ruler is not forever long and neither is the string. You are not your age forever, and neither is this calendar. All of them end.

But God says that all of his followers are going to live forever. Forever is a long time. As a matter of fact, there is no end to forever. It is further than we can see. It is longer than any street or, if you put all of the string together in the world, it would not be as long as forever. It is older than all of the years that anyone can live on earth, or if you added up all of the ages of all of the people that have ever lived.

That is why, when Jesus tells us that all of his followers are going to live forever with him and his Father in heaven, he means that we are never going to die in heaven. We will die here on earth just like everyone dies, but when we are brought back to life by God to live with God in heaven, then we shall never die. We will live forever.

The next time someone asks you how long your ruler is or if your string is as long as your front yard, I want you to think about what Jesus told us about how long we are going to live with God in heaven, and you will know that we are going to live forever. Amen.

What Keeps Us Running

John 6:60-69

It is the spirit that gives life, the flesh is of no avail; the words that I have spoken to you are spirit and life. (v. 63)

Object: *Some gasoline in a can.*

Good morning, boys and girls. Today I want to tell you a little bit about the spirit. How many of you have ever heard someone talk about "spirit," your spirit? *(Let them answer.)* That's good, it is a word that all of us have heard. How many of you know what I mean when I talk about your spirit? *(Let them answer.)* Those are pretty hard questions, aren't they? We have heard of our spirit and the Spirit of God, and we know that we have one, but it is very hard to talk about.

Let me try to show you what I think it could be like. How many of you have ever been in a car with your mom or dad when they were afraid that they were going to run out of gas? *(Let them answer.)* Almost all of us. It is a terrible feeling because you know what is going to happen if you run out of gas, don't you? *(Let them answer.)* Right, you are going to sit and wait until someone goes and gets some gas for the car. You may even have to walk for a long way to find some. It is an awful experience. Everything else about the car is all right but it won't run. Check the tires and you will see that they have plenty of air, or the engine and you will see that it is in fine shape; but without gas the car will not run. You must have gas. Nothing else will make it run. You could pour 500 gallons of water in the gas tank and it will not budge an inch. You must have gasoline.

That is the way it is with us as people. Our bodies can be great. We can have the best looking muscles in the world, but they are not the most important thing. You can have beautiful hair that reaches down to the middle of your back and that is not very important. You can have shiny teeth or big blue eyes, but you need something even more important to have a real life and that is "spirit." Jesus says that it is the spirit that gives life. Our muscles, hair, teeth, heart, legs are not as important to life as "spirit," and that is the one thing that God gives us. God gives us our spirit and in so doing he gives us life.

The next time you must get gas for your car to make it run, I hope that you think for a moment about the thing that God gives us to make us run, our spirit. We are very grateful to God for spirit and we thank him for it every day. Amen.

God's Good Gift

John 7:37-39

Now this he said about the Spirit, which those who believed in him were to receive; for as yet the Spirit had not been given, because Jesus was not yet glorified. (v. 39)

Object: *A ballot box and some ballots.*

Good morning, boys and girls. How many of you can think about one thing that you are not allowed to do? I want you to think a lot about that one thing and tell me why you are not allowed to do it? Is it because you are too small, or that you would get sick or hurt? There are usually good reasons why we are not allowed to do certain things. You are not allowed to rob banks or eat poison, because either you or someone else will be hurt by doing those things. I brought along with me something that you are not allowed to do because you are not old enough to do it. *(Bring out the ballot box.)* Do you know what this is? *(Let them answer.)* It is a ballot box and you use it when you vote. *(Show them a ballot.)* This is a ballot. It is where you mark whom you vote for. If you want to vote for the President of the United States you must be eighteen years old. You must be that old to vote for congressmen, or the mayor, or almost anything to do with government. There is a special age you must be before the government gives you the right to vote. To be able to vote is something that is given to you at just the right time of your life.

There are other things which are given. I like to remember

the story in the Bible that talks about the time that God gave the Holy Spirit to the people who believed in Jesus. It was a gift from God. God gives the Spirit. It is not something that we can buy or take or even make. It must be given by God.

The state or the nation gives you the right to vote, but only at a certain time in your life. You must be eighteen years old. That is not true about the Spirit of God. God gives the gift of the Spirit and God gives it to people at all ages. You may be a baby or you may be much older but the Spirit is given by God to people who believe that Jesus lived and died for them and finally was brought back to life after he was crucified. It is a wonderful gift that God has given to us who believe in Jesus. The Holy Spirit gives us power that we could not have in any other way. We should thank God for such a wonderful gift and pray to the Holy Spirit often, so that the power is shared with us. Just remember that the Holy Spirit is given to us by God and that it is not something that we can buy or make. Amen.

Jesus Knows

John 10:11-18

I am the good shepherd; I know my own and my own know me. (v. 14)

Object: *A growl. Ask all of the children to growl on cue.*

Good morning, boys and girls. Today we are going to learn something, and at the same time have a very good time doing it. How many of you have a dog for a pet? *(Let them raise their hands.)* Is your dog a good watchdog? *(Let them answer.)* He is a good watchdog. What does that mean? *(Let them answer.)* When someone comes to your house and knocks on the door or rings the doorbell, the dog barks or growls. Is there anyone here who can make the sound of a dog growling? *(Ask for a volunteer to do it first, and then ask everyone to join the volunteer in growling.)* That sounds great. As a matter of fact, it sounds kind of scary. I don't think I would want to come in your house if I heard that kind of noise on the other side of the door. Does a watchdog do this — make that growling noise — to everyone? *(Let them answer.)* Does your dog make that noise when he knows that you are coming home or if your parents come home? *(Let them answer.)* I don't think so. Most watch dogs growl only at strangers.

The reason I said this was because Jesus talked about himself as a shepherd to sheep. He called people his sheep and he said that he was a good shepherd. That means that he does more than just watch people. He really cares for people. The Bible says that Jesus knows the sheep. He knows us so well that he can call each of us by our name. Imagine that. Jesus knows us and loves us. He does things to make sure that we know how much he loves us. That is why we pray that he will be with us at night when we sleep, at all of our meals when we eat, while we are in school, or when we play. Jesus knows us. We are never a stranger to him like some people are to our watchdogs. He always knows us and what our need are. The next time you hear your watchdog growl at a stranger, I want you to remember that the reason your dog is growling is because he does not think that he knows the person who is coming to your house. When you remember that, I want you to also remember that it is not that way with Jesus. He knows us all and he knows us well. Will you remember that? Good. Amen.

Share It or Lose It

John 12:20-33

He who loves his life loses it, and he who hates his life in this world will keep it for eternal life. (v. 25)

Object: *Some bread, some milk, and some melted ice cream.*

Good morning, boys and girls. How many of you like to eat? *(Let them answer.)* What do you like to eat most? *(Let them answer.)* I like those things, too. Does anyone like milk? Good, that is really good for you. Does anyone like bread? That's good for you, too. How about ice cream? Everybody likes ice cream. Did you ever wish that you still had some ice cream to eat or some milk to drink after everything was all gone? *(Let them answer.)* I know a person who always likes to save his favorite food until everyone else has eaten theirs, and then he eats very slowly. He says that he just loves ice cream, and he can't stand it when it is all eaten. That's the way he feels. Of course, sometimes he is sorry. Sometimes he waits too long and then you know what happens. *(Show them the melted ice cream.)* He loved his ice cream too much.

We can love some things too much. We can love our own life too much. People try to save their lives so much that they never really do the kind of things that God gave us a life for. I know people who are so afraid that they will be hurt in an automobile accident that they never ride in a car. They sit at home and spoil. I know a boy who never plays baseball or football, because he is afraid that he will be hurt. He misses not only the game, but the fun of playing with others. God gave us a life to use and to use it all up. Your life and my life is like a glass of milk or a gallon of ice cream. It is meant to be used just like the milk should be drunk and the ice cream eaten. If we don't use our lives and give them to others, then they will spoil and get rotten, just like the food will spoil and become rotten.

Jesus told people a long time ago that the way we use our lives is really important to God and to us. People who are afraid to live will lose everything. People who are willing to share their lives and use them all up will have new lives with God forever. That is a promise that God makes to us. If you take this bread and set it on a counter and never eat it, then it will get hard as a rock before turning to dust and blow away. If you like your ice cream so much that you don't want to eat it, for fear that you will not have any more, then it will melt and finally evaporate. That means that the food that you liked the most has been lost, and has done no one any good. Use your life, give it to God and know the happiness that he has always wanted you to have. Amen.

Vines and Branches

John 15:1-8

I am the vine, you are the branches. He who abides in me, and I in him, he it is that bears much fruit, for apart from me you can do nothing. (v. 5)

Object: *A piece of vine for each child.*

Good morning, boys and girls. Today we are going to learn about another way that we belong to Jesus, and the way that Jesus cares for us. I know that all of you believe that Jesus cares for you, but I want to show you something that will help us to understand how he does it. How many of you have ever seen a vine like this? *(Show them a vine.)* I know that all of you have seen them at one time or another, but have you ever noticed how there is one main branch with a lot of smaller branches off the one main branch? *(Let them answer.)* Let's pretend that Jesus is the main branch and that we are the little branches. Now, it is the big branch that gives all of the strength to the little branches. Now, it is the big branch that gives all of the strength to the little branches. All of the food for the little branches comes through the big branch. Without it the little branches would shrivel up and die.

Jesus tells us that this is the same way he works with us. Because of Jesus, we have life. Without Jesus there would be no life. It is because of him that we have all of the good things, like rain and sunshine, trees and food, animals and birds, and all the other things that make up the world. Jesus also gives us love and forgiveness and each other. Everything that is good comes from the main branch called God.

There is only one other thing that needs to be said, but it is important. The more we love God and serve him, the closer we are to him. Jesus says that the closer we are, the more good things there will be for us. That is something to remember for we miss a lot of good things in this world because we are not closer to God. It is important that we remember who gives us our power and our strength and then stay close to him. Jesus says that the branches of the vine that are closest to the main branch have the most strength, and you and I can see that this is true. I want you to take your vine home and put it in some water until it grows some roots, and then plant it in the ground. You will always remember then the story that Jesus told about how he was the main branch and we are the little branches that comes from him. Will you do that? Wonderful! Amen.

Chosen by the Captain

John 15:9-17

You did not choose me, but I chose you and appointed you that you should go and bear fruit and that your fruit should abide; so that whatever you ask the Father in my name, he may give it to you. (v. 16)

Object: *A shirt with the word "captain" written on it.*

Good morning, boys and girls. Today we are going to learn a great lesson about the way that you and God became such great friends. Did you know that you were a great friend of God? *(Let them answer.)* Wonderful, all of you know that little piece of truth. Well, then, let me show you how you became such a good friend.

(Bring out the shirt with the word "captain" lettered on it.) How many of you can read the word written on the shirt? *(Let them read it.)* That's right, the word is CAPTAIN. Do you know what a captain is or does? *(Let them answer.)* That's right. All of those things tell us what a captain does. I suppose one of the most important things that a captain does is to make choices. Today he will choose a person to do a job. Tomorrow he must choose the color that he wants to paint his ship. To make choices is something that a captain must do, and a good captain makes good choices.

God is a great captain. God makes choices all of the time. One of the choices that God makes is a friend or a follower. God chooses people and, here comes the important part, he chose you. That's right, God chose you. You did not choose

God because you are not the captain. God is the only one who chooses people for his world, and for his eternal world, and you are one of them. Isn't that great? That's the way God works. He chooses people to be his friends and his followers, just as the captain of a boat chooses the work to be done and the people do it. God chose you just as the captain of a team chooses the people whom he wants to play on his team. God chooses you and me to be his followers and to work in his church.

The next time that you hear someone talking about captains and that a captain has to choose the people who are going to work or play with him, I want you to remember that God is a captain, too. When you remember that, then you will also remember that, since God is the Captain, he is also the one who chose you to be a part of his great team. If you remember that, you will have learned a very important lesson, that people are God's choice and not that God is the choice of people. Amen.

Guarding Us from Evil

John 17:11b-19

While I was with them, I kept them in thy name, which thou hast given me; I have guarded them, and none of them is lost but the son of perdition, that the scripture might be fulfilled. (v. 12)

Object: *A badge and strap that are used by the school patrol to watch children when they cross the street.*

Good morning, boys and girls. I have with me today something that I know every boy and girl who goes to school hopes to wear some day. *(Show them the symbol of the school guard.)* How many of you hope to wear this some day? A lot of you. What does someone do when they wear this at your school? *(Let them answer.)* That's right, they stand on the corner or at the place where children cross the street and stop the cars so that children can cross safely. That is a very important job because it makes it safe for the children to walk to school. One of the names used to describe this person who wears this is a traffic guard or a school guard. To guard someone means to take care of them or to watch over them.

Jesus talked about himself as a guard one night when he was praying to his Father in heaven. He told the Father that he had guarded all of the disciples that the Father had given him except the one who was betraying him. That one was Judas, and he killed himself. But Jesus felt that he had been asked to watch over and care for the other disciples and he had done so. Now the time had come for Jesus to go back to heaven and live with his Father, and he wanted the disciples to be cared for or guarded even after he left. That is why he prayed for them.

I think it is wonderful that Jesus felt like this about his disciples. I know that Jesus cares for all of us, but the eleven men who worked with him and followed him, even when they did not know what was happening, were a little special. Jesus knew they were special, and he felt a real big love for them, and he wanted the Father to know how he felt. So, Jesus prayed for them and talked about them in that way. That makes me feel good because I know now that Jesus may care that way about me or you or all of us. We are people who are not as smart as God, or as strong or brave as God, but we care what happens to us and to our friends and family. If Jesus cared that way about his disciples, then I know that he will have special feelings about other people like you and me who follow him, even when we do not understand everything that happens.

Maybe the next time you see a school guard or any person who is guarding someone else to keep them safe, you will remember the time that Jesus talked about himself guarding the disciples and how he showed his care for them. I know that he will show you the same care when he guards you. Amen.

Who's In Charge?

John 18:33-37

Jesus answered, "My kingship is not of this world; if my kingship were of this world my servants would fight, that I might not be handed over to the Jews; but my kingship is not from the world." *(v. 36)*

Object: *A gavel.*

Good morning, boys and girls. Today we are going to talk about kings and kingdoms. How many of you have ever met a king? *(Let them answer.)* Why not? Have you heard of kings? *(Let them answer.)* Of course you have heard of them, but we have very few kings left in the world and none of them are in this country. A king is a person who is in charge of his country. Once upon a time they made the laws and they made people obey the laws. People fought for their king and even died for him if they had to. A king was in charge of his country.

I brought with me this morning a tool that helps some people be in charge of other people. *(Show them the gavel.)* Do you know who uses one of these? *(Let them answer.)* That's right, a judge uses one of these, and so do presidents and committees. This shows that they are in charge of the meeting or the court. It is called a gavel, and it helps to keep order in a meeting. I don't know if a king used a gavel, but he probably used something like it to show that he was in charge.

Many people wanted to know if Jesus was a king, and if he was the king, was he in charge of them and their country.

Jesus tried to explain to them that he was a king, but not just their king. That didn't sound right to them. He lived with them, worked with them and ate with them. How could he do all of that and not be their king. He was a king, he said, but a different kind of king. They already had kings of their countries. Jesus was a king because the Father in Heaven made him the king over all the countries, all the people, and all the world. Jesus was the "king of men" who live a long time before they died, and he would be the king of men who lived after they lived. That is hard to understand. They wanted Jesus to either be their king, or no one's king. But Jesus knew about God's plan and how people were going to live forever with him in heaven. Jesus knew that men would need a king who did not love some people and hate other people. That was the kind of king that Jesus would be. Jesus did not want people to fight for him, and fight against other people. Jesus was the king of all the people and that was what he was trying to teach them. But they would not listen. They did not understand that he was the Son of God. *Now* we know what he meant. He was not going to be the king of some people for a little bit of time. Jesus is our king now, because he is in charge of our world, just like he has always been in charge. The next time you see a gavel, or you hear about a king, I want you to think about Jesus and how he is the king of the world for all time and for all people. Amen.

"Prove It"

John 20:19-31

But he (Thomas) said to them, "Unless I see in his hands the print of the nails, and place my finger in the marks of the nails, and place my hand in his side, I will not believe." (v. 25b)

Object: *Some nails, a hammer, some paper and wood.*

Good morning, boys and girls. How many of you know what I mean when I say "Prove it"? *(Let them answer.)* That's right, you want me to prove to you that what I say is true. If I say that I am six feet tall, then you want me to measure myself with a yardstick or a measuring tape. If I tell you that I weigh two hundred pounds and you don't believe me, you say: "Prove it." That means that I must get a scale and show you that I weigh two hundred pounds according to that scale.

The disciples of Jesus had an experience like this. One of them, Thomas, was not with them when Jesus came back and visited them. They told Thomas that Jesus was alive, but he didn't believe it. He said, "Prove it." They said that they had seen Jesus with their own eyes. Thomas told them that he would not believe Jesus was alive, unless he could see the holes in Jesus' hands where the nails had been driven in when the soldiers crucified him. Thomas really wanted the proof.

Now, I have a hammer with me and some nails. I am going to nail a piece of paper to some wood. The paper would be softer than Jesus' hands, but the wood is harder. After I nail this paper to the wood, I am going to take the nail out and we'll take a look at it. *(Nail the paper to the the wood several times.)* Now, let's take the nails out. *(Do it carefully.)* How about that? Thomas was right. If Jesus was nailed to a cross, there would be proof because the nails would have made holes in his hands, or anywhere else that the nails went into his body.

So, Thomas knew that, if the person whom they saw was really Jesus, he would have holes in him from the nails. He waited to see what would happen. This time he did not leave, but stayed with the other disciples. Then, a few days later, Jesus was standing with them. Thomas did not know where he came from, but there he was. And Jesus seemed to know that Thomas was waiting for proof. He held out his hands and pointed to his side where the soldiers had stabbed him with a spear and he asked Thomas to feel the places where the nails and spear had made the holes. Thomas didn't need to. He was sure that this was Jesus. He could see the holes, and there was no doubt that this was truly Jesus. That is what you really call "proving it."

Sometimes, today, people wonder if Jesus was really alive after he had died. If you have ever thought about this, then just read the story about Thomas and the day he asked Jesus to prove it to him. If you read it, you will believe that Jesus really did live after he died. That is the proof.

Whenever you see a nail, I hope you will remember the day that Thomas asked for proof and Jesus gave it to him. Will you do that? That's good. Amen.